INTRODUCTION TO PROBLEM SOLVING USING C PROGRAMMING

C PROGRAMMING LANGUAGE

GOKUL.K

I sincerely thanks to my beloved principal sir Dr.A.Palaniappan fully encourageing and Motivated my selfand I Thanks to My Friends to Finding the Correct way of Expose My self Knowledge

Contents

Foreword

C is a general-purpose programming language created by Dennis Ritchie at the Bell Laboratories in 1972. It is a very popular language, despite being old. C is strongly associated with UNIX, as it was developed to write the UNIX operating system.

Basically, C is a collection of its library functions. It is also flexible to add user-defined functions and include those in the C library.

* Simple and Efficient. The basic syntax style of implementing C language is very simple and easy to learn. ...

* Dynamic Memory Management,Modularity With Structured Language,Mid-Level Programming Language.

Preface

This book is devoted to practical C programming. C is currently the premier language for software developers. That's because it's widely distributed and standard. Newer languages are available, such as C++, but these are still evolving. C is still the language of choice for robust, portable programming.

This book emphasizes the skills you will need to do real-world programming. It teaches you not only the mechanics of the C language, but the entire life cycle of a C program as well (including the program's conception, design, code, methods, debugging, release, documentation, maintenance, and revision).

Good style is emphasized. To create a good program you must do more than just type in code. It is an art in which writing and programming skills blend themselves together to form a masterpiece. True art can be created. A well-written program not only functions correctly, but is simple and easy to understand. Comments allow the programmer to include descriptive text inside the program. When clearly written, a commented program is highly prized.

A program should be as simple as possible. A programmer should avoid clever tricks. This book stresses simple, practical rules

Acknowledgements

I would like to express my greatest appreciation to the all individuals who have helped and supported me throughout the Book. I am thankful to my Principal for his ongoing support during the Book, from initial advice, and encouragement, which led to the final report of this Book.

Prologue

What Does C Programming Language (C) Mean? C is a high-level and general-purpose programming language that is ideal for developing firmware or portable applications. Originally intended for writing system software, C was developed at Bell Labs by Dennis Ritchie for the Unix Operating System in the early 1970s

C is a powerful general-purpose programming language. It can be used to develop software like operating systems, databases, compilers, and so on.

CHAPTER ONE

Introduction

Basic Concepts of Computer

Computer is an electronic device which is used to store the data, as per given instructions it gives results quickly and accurately.

i. Data : Data is a raw material of information.
v. Information : Proper collection of the data is called information.

Characteristics of Computer

1. Speed: - As you know computer can work very fast. It takes only few seconds for calculations that we take hours to complete. You will be surprised to know that computer can perform millions (1,000,000) of instructions and even more per second. Therefore, we determine the speed of computer in terms of microsecond.
2. Accuracy: - The degree of accuracy of computer is very high and every calculation is performed with the same accuracy. The accuracy level is 7. determined on the basis of design of computer. The errors in computer are due to human and inaccurate data.
3. Diligence: - A computer is free from tiredness, lack of concentration, fatigue, etc. It can work for hours without creating any error. If millions of calculations are to be performed, a computer will perform every calculation with the same accuracy. Due to this capability it overpowers human being

in routine type of work.

4. Versatility: - It means the capacity to perform completely different type of work. You may use your computer to prepare payroll slips. Next moment you may use it for inventory management or to prepare electric bills.
5. Power of Remembering: - Computer has the power of storing any amount of information or data. Any information can be stored and recalled as long as you require it, for any numbers of years. It depends entirely upon you how much data you want to store in a computer and when to lose or retrieve these data.
6. No IQ: - Computer is a dumb machine and it cannot do any work without instruction from the user. It performs the instructions at tremendous speed and with accuracy. It is you to decide what you want to do and in what sequence. So a computer cannot take its own decision as you can.
7. Storage: - The Computer has an in-built memory where it can store a large amount of data. You can also store data in secondary storage devices such as floppies, which can be kept outside your computer and can be carried to other computers.

Uses of Computers

Education : Getting the right kind of information is a major challenge as is getting information to make sense. College students spend an average of 5-6 hours a week on the internet. Research shows that computers can significantly enhance performance in learning. This offers a variety of internet and video-based online courses.

Health and Medicine : Computer technology is radically changing the tools of medicine. All medical information can now be digitized. Software is now able to computer the risk of a disease. Mental health researchers are using computers to screen troubled teenagers in need of psychotherapy. A patient paralyzed by a stroke has received an implant that allows communication between his brain and a computer; as a result, he can move a cursor across a screen by brainpower and convey simple messages.

Science : Scientists have long been users of it. A new adventure among scientists is the idea of a "collaboratory", an internet based collaborative laboratory, in which researchers all over the world can work easily together even at a distance. An example is space physics where space physicists are allowed to band together to measure the earth"s ionosphere from instruments on four parts of the world.

Business : Business clearly see the interest as a way to enhance productivity and competitiveness. Some areas of business that are undergoing rapid changes are sales and marketing, retailing, banking, stock trading, etc. Sales representatives not only need to be better educated and more knowledgeable about their customer"s businesses, but also must be comfortable with computer technology. The internet has become a popular marketing tool. The world of cybercash has come to banking – not only smart cards but internet banking, electronic deposit, bill paying, online stock and bond trading, etc.

Government: Various departments of the Government use computer for their planning, control and law enforcement activities. To name a few – Traffic, Tourism, Information & Broadcasting, Education, Aviation and many others.

Defence: There are many uses computers in Defence such as:

- Controlling UAV or unmanned air-crafts an example is Predator. If you have cable I would recommend watching the shows "Future Weapons" and "Modern Marvels". The show future weapon gives an entire hour to the predator.
- They are also used on Intercontinental Ballistic Missiles (ICBMs) that uses GPS and Computers to help the missile get to the target.
- Computers are used to track incoming missiles and help slew weapons systems onto the incoming target to destroy them.

Sports: In today's technologically growing society, computers are being used in nearly every activity.

Recording Information : Official statistics keepers and some scouts use computers to record statistics, take notes and chat online while attending and working at a sports event.

Analyzing Movements : The best athletes pay close attention to detail. Computers can slow recorded video and allow people to study their specific movements to try to improve their tendencies and repair poor habits.

TYPES OF COMPUTERS or Classification of Computers

1. **Super Computers**
2. **Main Frame Computers**
3. **Mini Computers**
4. **Micro Computers**

1. **Super Computers** are the most powerful computers in terms of speed of execution and large storage capacity. NASA uses supercomputers to track and control space explorations.

E.g.:- CRAY Research :- CRAY-1 & CRAY-2, Fujitsu (VP2000), Hitachi (S820), NEC (SX20),

PARAM 10000 by C-DAC, Anupam by BARC, PACE Series by DRDO

? Most powerful Computer system - needs a large room

? Minimum world length is 64 bits

? CPU speed: 100 MIPS

? Equivalent to 4000 computers

? High cost: 4 – 5 millions

? Able to handle large amount of data

? High power consumption

? High precision

Applications

? In petroleum industry - to analyze volumes of seismic data which are gathered during oil seeking explorations to identify areas where there is possibility of getting petroleum products inside the earth

? In Aerospace industry - to simulate airflow around an aircraft at different speeds and altitude.

This helps in producing an effective aerodynamic design for superior performance

? In Automobile industry – to do crash simulation of the design of an automobile before it is released for manufacturing – for better automobile design

2. **Mainframe Computers** Are next to supercomputers in terms of capacity. The mainframe computers are multi terminal computers, which can be shared simultaneously by multiple users. Unlike personal computers, mainframe computers offer time-sharing For example, insurance companies use mainframe computers to process information about millions of its policyholders.[E.g.:- IBM 3000 series, Burroughs B7900, Univac 1180, DEC]

? Supports multi-user facility

? Number of processors varies from one to six.

? Cost: 3500 to many million dollars

? Kept in air conditioned room to keep them cool

? Supports many I/O and auxiliary storage devices

? Supports network of terminals

Applications

? Used to process large amount of data at very high speed such as in the case of Banks/ Insurance Companies/ Hospitals/ Railways...which need online processing of large number of transactions and requires massive data storage and processing capabilities

? Used as controlling nodes in WANs (Wide Area Networks)

? Used to mange large centralized databases

3. **Minicomputers** These computers are also known as midrange computers. These are desk-sized machines and are used in medium scale applications. For example, production

departments use minicomputers to monitor various manufacturing processes and assembly- line operations.

E.g.:- Digital Equipments PDP 11/45 and VAX 11)
? Perform better than micros
? Large in size and costlier than micros
? Designed to support more than one user at a time
? Posses large storage capacities and operates at higher speed
? Support faster peripheral devices like high speed printers

Applications

? These computers are used when the volume of processing is large for e.g. Data processing for a medium sized organization
? Used to control and monitor production processes
? To analyze results of experiments in laboratories
? Used as servers in LANs (Local Area Networks)

4. **Microcomputers** As compared to supercomputers, mainframes and minicomputers, microcomputers are the least powerful. It is having single processor but these are very widely used and rapidly gaining in popularity. It comprises of a keyboard, mouse, monitor and system unit. The system unit is also known as cabinet or chassis. It is the container that houses most of the components such as motherboard, disk drives, ports, switch mode power supply and add-on cards etc. The desktop computers are available in two models- horizontal model and tower model.

Applications

Used in the field of desktop publishing, accounting, statistical analysis, graphic designing, investment analysis, project management, teaching, entertainment etc

? The different models of microcomputers are given below:-

a. **Personal computers**:- The name PC was given by the IBM for its microcomputers. PCs are used for word processing, spreadsheet calculations, database management etc.

b. **Note book or Lap Top**:- Very small in terms of size – can be folded and carried around – Monitor is made up of LCD and the keyboard and system units are contained in a single box. Got all the facilities of a personal computer (HDD, CDD, Sound card, N/W card, Modem etc) and a special connection to connect to the desktop PC which can be used to transfer data.

GENERATION OF COMPUTERS

The first electronic computer was designed and built at the University of Pennsylvania based on vacuum tube technology. Vacuum tubes were used to perform logic operations and to store data. Generations of computers has been divided into five according to the development of technologies used to fabricate the processors, memories and I/O units.

I. **Generation : 1945 – 55**
II. **Generation : 1955 – 65**
III. **Generation : 1965 – 75**
IV. **Generation : 1975 – 89**
V. **Generation : 1989 to present**

First Generation (ENIAC - Electronic Numerical Integrator And Calculator EDSAC – Electronic Delay Storage Automatic Calculator EDVAC – Electronic Discrete Variable Automatic Computer UNIVAC – Universal Automatic Computer

IBM 701)

? Vacuum tubes were used – basic arithmetic operations took few milliseconds

? Bulky

? Consume more power with limited performance

? High cost

? Uses assembly language – to prepare programs. These were translated into machine level language for execution.

? Mercury delay line memories and Electrostatic memories were used

? Fixed point arithmetic was used

? 100 to 1000 fold increase in speed relative to the earlier mechanical and relay based electromechanical technology

? Punched cards and paper tape were invented to feed programs and data and to get results.

? Magnetic tape / magnetic drum were used as secondary memory

? Mainly used for scientific computations.

Second Generation (Manufacturers – IBM 7030, Digital Data Corporation"s PDP 1/5/8 Honeywell 400)

? Transistors were used in place of vacuum tubes. (invented at AT&T Bell lab in 1947)

? Small in size

? Lesser power consumption and better performance

? Lower cost

? Magnetic ferrite core memories were used as main memory which is a random-access nonvolatile memory

? Magnetic tapes and magnetic disks were used as secondary memory

? Hardware for floating point arithmetic operations was developed.

? Index registers were introduced which increased flexibility of programming.

? High level languages such as FORTRAN, COBOL etc were used - Compilers were developed to translate the high-level program into corresponding assembly language program which was then translated into machine language.

? 1000 fold increase in speed.

? Increasingly used in business, industry and commercial organizations for preparation of payroll, inventory control, marketing, production planning, research, scientific & engineering analysis and design etc.

Third Generation (System 360 Mainframe from IBM, PDP-8 Mini Computer from Digital Equipment Corporation)

? ICs were used

? Small Scale Integration and Medium Scale Integration technology were implemented in CPU, I/O processors etc.

? Smaller & better performance ? Comparatively lesser cost ? Faster processors

? In the beginning magnetic core memories were used. Later they were replaced by semiconductor memories (RAM & ROM)

? Introduced microprogramming

? Microprogramming, parallel processing (pipelining, multiprocessor system etc), multiprogramming, multi-user system (time shared system) etc were introduced.

? Operating system software were introduced (efficient sharing of a computer system by several user programs)

? Cache and virtual memories were introduced (Cache memory makes the main memory appear faster than it really is. Virtual memory makes it appear larger)

? High level languages were standardized by ANSI eg. ANSI FORTRAN, ANSI COBOL etc

? Database management, multi-user application, online systems like closed loop process control, airline reservation, interactive query systems, automatic industrial control etc emerged during this period.

Fourth Generation (Intel"s 8088,80286,80386,80486 .., Motorola"s 68000, 68030, 68040, Apple II, CRAY I/2/X/MP etc)

? Microprocessors were introduced as CPU– Complete processors and large section of main memory could be implemented in a single chip

? Tens of thousands of transistors can be placed in a single chip (VLSI design implemented)

? CRT screen, laser & ink jet printers, scanners etc were developed.

? Semiconductor memory chips were used as the main memory.

? Secondary memory was composed of hard disks – Floppy disks & magnetic tapes were used for backup memory

? Parallelism, pipelining cache memory and virtual memory were applied in a better way

? LAN and WANS were developed (where desktop work stations interconnected)

? Introduced C language and Unix OS

? Introduced Graphical User Interface

? Less power consumption

? High performance, lower cost and very compact

? Much increase in the speed of operation

Fifth Generation (IBM notebooks, Pentium PCs-Pentium 1/2/3/4/Dual core/Quad core.. SUN work stations, Origin 2000, PARAM 10000, IBM SP/2)

? Generation number beyond IV, have been used occasionally to describe some current computer system that have a dominant organizational or application driven feature.

? Computers based on artificial intelligence are available

? Computers use extensive parallel processing, multiple pipelines, multiple processors etc

? Massive parallel machines and extensively distributed system connected by communication networks fall in this category.

? Introduced ULSI (Ultra Large Scale Integration) technology – Intel"s Pentium 4 microprocessor contains 55 million transistors millions of components on a single IC chip.

? Superscalar processors, Vector processors, SIMD processors, 32 bit micro controllers and embedded processors, Digital Signal Processors (DSP) etc have been developed.

? Memory chips up to 1 GB, hard disk drives up to 180 GB and optical disks up to 27 GB are available (still the capacity is increasing)

? Object oriented language like JAVA suitable for internet programming has been developed.

? Portable note book computers introduced

? Storage technology advanced – large main memory and disk storage available

? Introduced World Wide Web. (and other existing applications like e-mail, e Commerce, Virtual libraries/Classrooms, multimedia applications etc.)

Basic Computer Organization

Basic Elements of Computer System Basic elements of a computer system are Mouse, Keyboard, monitor, memory, CPU, motherboard, Hard Disk, Speakers, Modem, power supply and processor. Computer Organization The block diagram of computer is shown in Fig. 1.1.

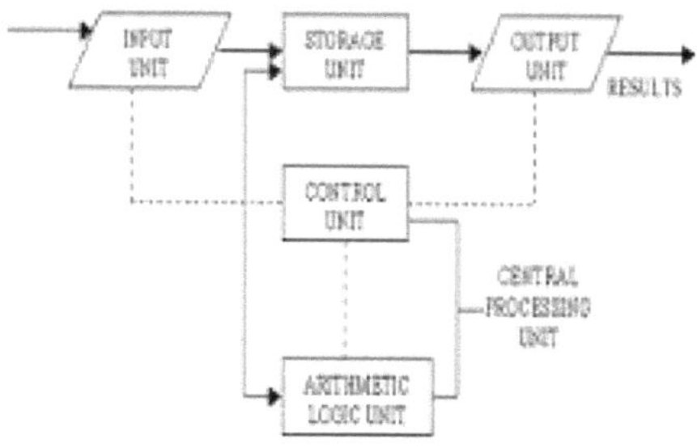

Basic Computer Organization

The computer performs basically five major operations of functions irrespective of their size and make. These are 1) it accepts data or instruction by way of input, 2) it stores data, 3) it can process data as required by the user, 4) it gives results in the form of output, and 5) it controls all operations inside a computer. We discuss below each of these operations.

INPUT UNIT

Input unit accepts coded information from human operators through electromechanical devices such as the keyboard or from other computers over digital communication lines. The keyboard is wired so that whenever a key is pressed, the corresponding letter or digit is automatically translated into its corresponding code and sent directly to either the memory or the processor.

RAM is the primary memory of the computer. It can be used every time of computer process the instruction. It is an active memory of the system. It holds the data temporarily. It works high speed than other memory. However we are using RAM.

- Contains a large number of semiconductor cells each capable of storing one bit of information
- These cells are processed in group of fixed size called words containing „n" bits. The main memory is organized such that the contents of one word can be stored or retrieved in one basic operation.
- For accessing data, a distinct address is associated with each word location.
- Data and programs must be in the primary memory for execution.

PROCESSOR UNIT

- The heart of the computer system is the Processor unit.
- It consists of Arithmetic and Logic Unit and Control Unit.

Arithmetic and Logic Unit (ALU)

- Most computer operations (Arithmetical and logical) are executed in ALU of the processor.
- For example: Suppose two numbers (operands) located in the main memory are to be added. These operands are brought into arithmetic unit – actual addition is carried. The result is then stored in the memory or retained in the processor itself for immediate use.
- Note that all operands may not reside in the main memory. Processor contains a number of high speed storage elements called Registers, which may be used for temporary storage of

frequently used operands. Each register can store one word of data.

- Access times to registers are 5 to 10 times faster than access time to memory.

Control Unit

- The operations of all the units are coordinated by the control unity (act as the nerve centre that sends control signal to other units)
- Timing signal that governs the I/O transfers are generated by the Control Unit.
- Synchronization signals are also generated by the Control Unit

By selecting, interpreting and executing the program instructions the program instructions the control unit is able to maintain order and direct the operation of the entire system

Storage Devices

Hard Disk, DVD, Pen Drive are the storage devices. It holds the data even switch off the computer. So it is called as permanent memory.

Hard Disk: Hard disk is used to store data permanently on computer.

Optical Disks: The Optical Disks are also called as the CD-ROM"s means Compact Disk Read Only Memory DVD means Digital Versatile Disk which is also used for Storing the data into the Disk and this is called as the Optical Disk.

CD – 700 MB DVD – 4.7 GB / 8.5 GB storage capacity.

Planning the Computer Program

Two write a correct program, a programmer must write each and every instruct in the correct sequence

i. Logic (instruction sequence) of a program can be very complex

v. Hence, programs must be planned before they are written to ensure program instruction are:

- Appropriate for the problem
- In the correct sequence

Stages of Problem Solving

1. Understand the problem
2. Define the problem

- given(s), goal, ownership, resources and constraints
- Given(s) = the initial situation
- Goal = Desired target situation
- Ownership = who does what
- Resources and constraints = tools, knowledge, skills, materials and rules, regulations, guidelines, boundaries, timings

3. Define boundaries
4. Plan solution.
5. Check solution

Debugging

Debugging is the process of finding and resolving defects or problems within a computer program that prevent correct operation of computer software or a system.

Debugging tactics can involve interactive debugging, control flow analysis, unit testing, integration testing, log file analysis, monitoring at the application or system level, memory dumps, and profiling.

Types of program errors

We distinguish between the following types of errors:

1. **Syntax errors**: errors due to the fact that the syntax of the language is not respected.
2. **Semantic errors**: errors due to an improper use of program statements.
3. **Logical errors**: errors due to the fact that the specification is not respected.

From the point of view of when errors are detected, we distinguish:

1. **Compile time errors**: syntax errors and static semantic errors indicated by the compiler.
2. **Runtime errors**: dynamic semantic errors, and logical errors, that cannot be detected by the compiler (debugging).

Top-down Design

A top-down approach (also known as stepwise design) is essentially the breaking down of a system to gain insight into the sub-systems that make it up. In a top-down approach an overview of the system is formulated, specifying but not detailing any first- level subsystems. Each subsystem is then refined in yet greater detail, sometimes in many additional subsystem levels, until the entire specification is reduced to base elements.

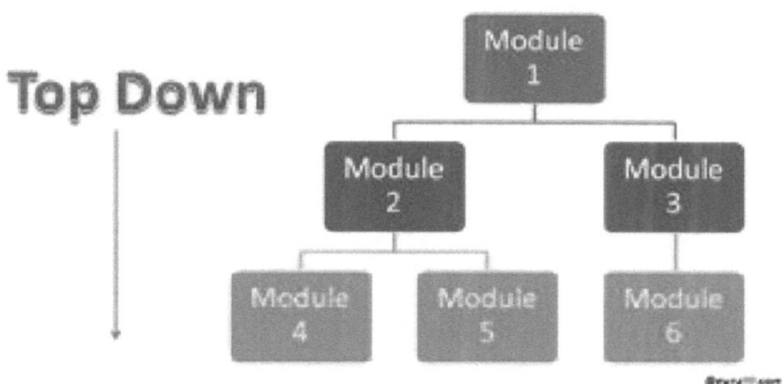

Top-down Design

Algorithm

Refers to the logic of a problem and a step-by-step description of how to arrive at the solution of a given problem. In order to qualify as an algorithm, a sequence of instruct must have following characteristics:

i. Each and every instruction should be precise and unambiguous

v. Each instruction should be such that it can be performed in a finite time.

One or more instructions should not be repeated infinitely, This ensures that the algorithm will ultimately terminate

Example : Algorithm for Simple Interest Step 1 : Start

Step 2 : Read p,n,r

Step 3 : Calculate si= p * n * r /100 Step 4 : Print si

Step 5 : Stop

Flowchart is a pictorial representation of an algorithm. The following table shows flowchart symbol and it"s usage.

Symbol	Name	Function
	Process	Indicates any type of internal operation inside the Processor or Memory
	input/output	Used for any Input / Output (I/O) operation. Indicates that the computer is to obtain data or output results
	Decision	Used to ask a question that can be answered in a binary format (Yes/No, True/False)
	Connector	Allows the flowchart to be drawn without intersecting lines or without a reverse flow.
	Predefined Process	Used to invoke a subroutine or an Interrupt program.
	Terminal	Indicates the starting or ending of the program, process, or interrupt program
	Flow Lines	Shows direction of flow.

Flowchart is a pictorial representation of an algorithm. The following table shows flowchart symbol and it"s usage.

Structured programming is a programming paradigm aimed at improving the clarity, quality, and development time of a computer program by making extensive use of the structured control flow constructs of selection (if/then/else) and repetition (while and for), block structures, and subroutines. Following the structured program theorem, all programs are seen as composed of control structures:

i. "Sequence"; ordered statements or subroutines executed in sequence.
v. "Selection"; one or a number of statements is executed depending on the state of the program. This is usually expressed with keywords such as if..then..else..endif.
v. "Iteration"; a statement or block is executed until the program reaches a certain state, or operations have been applied to every element of a collection. This is usually expressed with keywords such as while, repeat, for or do..until. Often it is recommended that each loop should only have one entry point (and in the original structural programming, also only one exit point, and a few languages enforce this).

CHAPTER TWO

C-Algorithms

C-Algorithms

In programming, algorithm are the set of well defined instruction in sequence to solve a program. An algorithm should always have a clear stopping point.

Write an algorithm to add two numbers entered by user.

Step 1: Start

Step 2: Declare variables num1, num2 and sum. Step 3: Read values num1 and num2.

Step 4: Add num1 and num2 and assign the result to sum. sum = num1+num2

Step 5: Display sum

Step 6: Stop

Pseudocode

Pseudocode typically omits details that are essential for machine understanding of the algorithm, such as variable declarations, system-specific code and some subroutines. The programming language is augmented with natural language description details, where convenient, or with compact mathematical notation.

C - PROGRAM STRUCTURE

A C program basically consists of the following parts:

- Preprocessor Commands
- Functions
- Variables
- Statements & Expressions

- Comments

Let us look at a simple code that would print the words "Hello World": #include <stdio.h>

```
int main()
{
/* my first program in C */ printf("Hello, World! \n");
return 0;
}
```

1. The first line of the program #include <stdio.h> is a preprocessor command, which tells a C compiler to include stdio.h file before going to actual compilation.
2. The next line int main() is the main function where the program execution begins.
3. The next line /*...*/ will be ignored by the compiler and it has been put to add additional comments in the program. So such lines are called comments in the program.

1. The next line printf(...) is another function available in C which causes the message "Hello, World!" to be displayed on the screen. 5. The next line return 0; terminates the main() function and returns the value 0.

Control Structures- if Selection Statement

In decision control statements (if-else and nested if), group of statements are executed when condition is true. If condition is false, then else part statements are executed.

There are 3 types of decision making control statements in C language. They are, if statements

if else statements nested if statements

<u>**Simple if statements**</u>

Syntax for each C decision control statements are if (condition)

{

Statements;

```
}
```

In these type of statements, if condition is true, then respective block of code is executed.

Example

```
void main()
{
int m=40,n=40; if (m == n)
{
printf("m and n are equal");
}
}
```

if ... else statements

In these type of statements, group of statements are executed when condition is true. If condition is false, then else part statements are executed.

Syntax:

```
if (condition)
{ Statement1; Statement2; } else
{ Statement3; Statement4; }
```

Example

```
#include <stdio.h> void main()
{
int m=40,n=20; if (m == n)
{
printf("m and n are equal");
}
else
{
printf("m and n are not equal");
}
}
```

Nested If statements

If condition 1 is false, then condition 2 is checked and statements are executed if it is true. If condition 2 also gets failure, then else part is executed.

Syntax:

```
if (condition1){ Statement1; } else_if(condition2)
{ Statement2; } else Statement 3;
```

Example

```
#include <stdio.h> void main()
{
int m=40,n=20; if (m>n) {
printf("m is greater than n");
}
else if(m<n) {
printf("m is less than n");
}
else {
printf("m is equal to n");
}
}
```

Loop control statements

Loop control statements in C are used to perform looping operations until the given condition is true. Control comes out of the loop statements once condition becomes false. There are 3 types of loop control statements in C language. They are,

1. for
2. while
3. do-while

1. for loop

for loop is a statement which allows code to be repeatedly executed. For loop contains 3 parts Initialization, Condition and Increment or Decrements.

Syntax

```
for (exp1; exp2; expr3)
{
statements;
```

```
}
```

Example

```
void main()
{
int i; clrscr();
for(i=1;i<5;i++)
{
printf("\n%d",i);
}
getch();
}
```

2. **do...while() loop**

A do-while loop is similar to a while loop, except that a do-while loop is execute at least one time.

A do while loop is a control flow statement that executes a block of code at least once, and then repeatedly executes the block, or not, depending on a given condition at the end of the block (in while).

Syntax

```
do { statements;
}while (condition);
```

Example

```
void main()
{
int i; i=1;
do
{
printf("\n%d",i); i++;
}while(i<5);
getch(); }
```

break and continue statements

C provides two commands to control how we loop:

- break -- exit form loop or switch.
- continue -- skip 1 iteration of loop.

You already have seen example of using break statement. Here is an example showing usage of **continue** statement.

```
#include main()
{
int i;
for( i = 0; i <= 5; i ++ )
{
if( i == 3 )
{
continue;
}
printf("Hello %d\n", i );
}
}
```

Output

```
Hello 0
Hello 1
Hello 2
Hello 4
Hello 5
```

In the above program when i value is 3 then control goes to the for loop again however it skip the printf statement.

Logical operators

C language supports following 3 logical operators. Suppose a=1 and b=0

We have three major logical operators in the C language – Logical NOT (!), Logical OR (||), and Logical AND (&&). The Logical NOT (!) Operator returns true whenever the conditions that are under condition are not at all satisfied.

Decision Making Statements In C: Modulus Op...

Operators In C: Array Of Pointers In C

Size Of Data Types In C: Data Types In C

Function In C: Difference Between Structured ..

ry the following example to understand all the logical operators available in C

```
#include <stdio.h>
main()
{
int a = 5; int b = 20; int c ;
if ( a && b )
{
printf("Line 1 - Condition is true\n" );
}
if ( a || b )
{
printf("Line 2 - Condition is true\n" );
} /* lets change the value of a and b */ a = 0; b = 10; if ( a && b )
{
printf("Line 3 - Condition is true\n" );
}
else
{
printf("Line 3 - Condition is not true\n" );
}
if ( !(a && b) )
{
printf("Line 4 - Condition is true\n" );
}
}
```

When you compile and execute the above program, it produces the following result –

```
Line 1 - Condition is true Line
2 - Condition is true
Line 3 - Condition is not true
Line 4 - Condition is true
```

What are the 3 logical operators?

There are three logical operators: and , or , and not . The semantics (meaning) of these operators is similar to their meaning in English.

Logical Operators

Operator	Meaning	Example	Result
&&	Logical and	(5<2)&&(5>3)	False
||	Logical or	(5<2)||(5>3)	True
!	Logical not	!(5<2)	True

C - Scope of variable

A scope in any programming is a region of the program where a defined variable can have its existence and beyond that variable it cannot be accessed. There are three places where variables can be declared in C programming language –

- Inside a function or a block which is called local variables.
- Outside of all functions which is called global variables.
- In the definition of function parameters which are called formalparameters.

Let us understand what are local and global variables, and formalparameters.

Local Variables

Variables that are declared inside a function or block are called local variables. They can be used only by statements that are inside that function or block of code. Local variables are not known to functions outside their own. The following example shows how local variables are used. Here all the variables a, b, and c are local to main() function.

Global Variables

Global variables are defined outside a function, usually on top of the program. Global variables hold their values throughout the lifetime of your program and they can be accessed inside any of the functions defined for the program.

A global variable can be accessed by any function. That is, a global variable is available for use throughout your entire program after its declaration. The following program show how global variables are used in a program.

```
#include <stdio.h>
/* global variable declaration */
int g;
void main () {
/* local variable declaration */ int a, b;
/* actual initialization */ a = 10;
b = 20;
g = a + b;
printf ("value of a = %d, b = %d and g = %d\n", a, b, g);
}
```

CHAPTER THREE

Functions

C - Functions

A function is a group of statements that together perform a task. Every C program has at least one function, which is main(), and all the most trivial programs can define additional functions.

You can divide up your code into separate functions. How you divide up your code among different functions is up to you, but logically the division is such that each function performs a specific task.

A function declaration tells the compiler about a function's name, return type, and parameters. A function definition provides the actual body of the function.

Defining a Function

The general form of a function definition in C programming language is as follows – return_type function_name(parameter list){

body of the function

}

A function definition in C programming consists of a function header and a function body. Here are all the parts of a function –

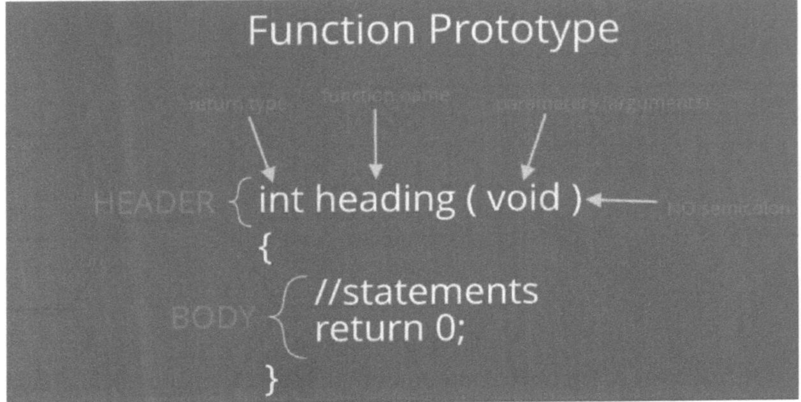

Enter Caption

Return Type – A function may return a value. The return_type is the data type of the value the function returns. Some functions perform the desired operations without returning a value. In this case, the return_type is the keyword void.

Function Name – This is the actual name of the function. The function name and the parameter list together constitute the function signature.

Parameters – A parameter is like a placeholder. When a function is invoked, you pass a value to the parameter. This value is referred to as actual parameter or argument. The

parameter list refers to the type, order, and number of the parameters of a function. Parameters are optional; that is, a function may contain no parameters.

Function Body – The function body contains a collection of statements that define what the function does.

Example

Given below is the source code for a function called max(). This function takes two parameters num1 and num2 and returns the maximum value between the two –

/* function returning the max between two numbers */ int max(int num1, int num2) {

/* local variable declaration */ int result;

if (num1 > num2) result = num1;

else

result = num2; return result;

}

Function Arguments

If a function is to use arguments, it must declare variables that accept the values of the arguments. These variables are called the formal parametersof the function.

Formal parameters behave like other local variables inside the function and are created upon entry into the function and destroyed upon exit.

While calling a function, there are two ways in which arguments can be passed to a function –

the arguments can be passed to a function in two ways, Call by value and call by reference. The actual parameter is passed to a function. A new memory area created for the passed parameters can be used only within the function. The actual parameters cannot be modified here.

Function declaration :

void function();

Function call : function();

Function definition : void function()

{

statements;

}

```
// C code for function with no
// arguments and no return value
#include <stdio.h>
void value(void);
void main()
{
value();
```

```
}
void value(void)
{
float year = 1, period = 5, amount = 5000, inrate = 0.12;
float sum;
sum = amount;
while (year <= period) {
sum = sum * (1 + inrate);
year = year + 1;
}
printf(" The total amount is %f:", sum);
}
```

From the above two program notice that each time „countdown()" is called recursively, formal integer argument „count" is created and it obtained copy of integer from previous recursive call of function „countdown()". Therefore, there were created 101 integers with same name „count", last one with value 0. Each „count" is private/local to its function and so there"s no same name conflict. We know in C that when a function is called, it"s allotted a portion of temporary area called STACK for placing up there its private/local arguments, return addresses of calling functions etc. This way, for 101 recursive function calls to itself, there were created 101 STACKS, one for each function. Further, this caused recursion slow. Also, recursion exhausts systems important memory resources and might cause the program to abnormally aborted.

Array

An array is a collection of data that holds fixed number of values of same type. For example: if you want to store marks of 100 students, you can create an array for it.

```
int mark[100];
```

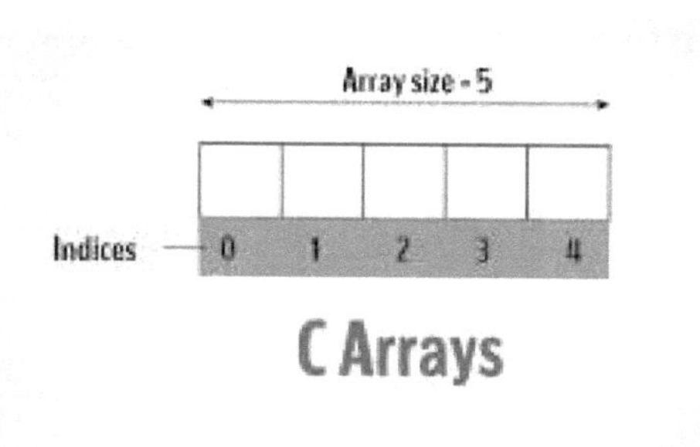

Enter Caption

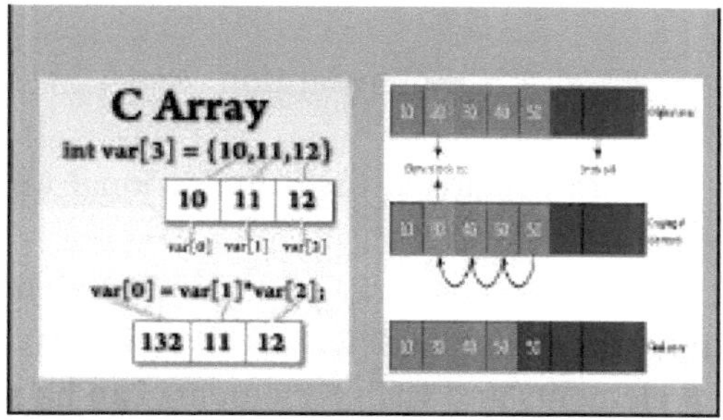

Enter Caption

Arrays are of two types:

One-dimensional arrays

int mark[5] = {19, 10, 8, 17, 9};

Arrays have 0 as the first index not 1. In this example, mark[0]

If the size of an array is n, to access the last element, (n-1) index is used. In this example, mark[4]

Multidimensional arrays

In C programming, you can create an array of arrays known as multidimensional array. For example,

float x[3][4];

Here, x is a two-dimensional (2d) array. The array can hold 12 elements. You can think the array as table with 3 row and each row has 4 column.

	Column 1	Column 2	Column 3	Column 4
Row 1	x[0][0]	x[0][1]	x[0][2]	x[0][3]
Row 2	x[1][0]	x[1][1]	x[1][2]	x[1][3]
Row 3	x[2][0]	x[2][1]	x[2][2]	x[2][3]

Enter Caption

Similarly, you can declare a three-dimensional (3d) array. For example,

float y[2][4][3]; Here,The array y can hold 24 elements

You can think this example as: Each 2 elements have 4 elements, which makes 8 elements and each 8 elements can have 3 elements. Hence, the total number of elements is 24.

Passing array to function

While passing arrays as arguments to the function, only the name of the array is passed. C program to pass an array containing age of person to a function. This function should find average age and display the average age in main function.

```
#include <stdio.h>
float average(float age[]);
int main()
{
float avg, age[] = { 23.4, 55, 22.6, 3, 40.5, 18 };
avg = average(age); /* Only name of array is passed as argument.
*/ printf("Average age=%.2f", avg);
return 0;
```

```
}
float average(float age[])
{
int i;
float avg, sum = 0.0; for (i = 0; i < 6; ++i) {
sum += age[i];
}
avg = (sum / 6); return avg;
}
```

Sorting Array

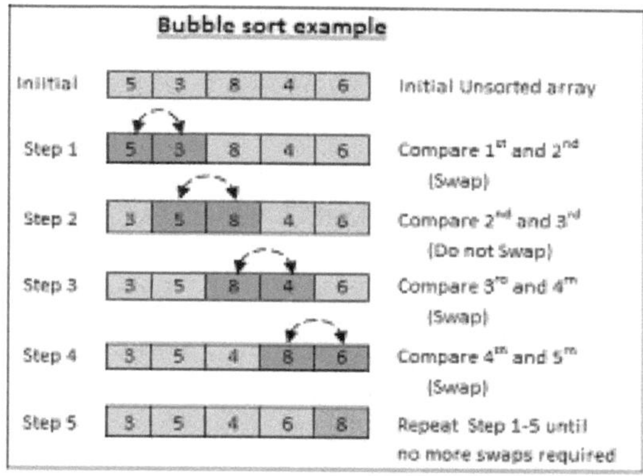

Enter Caption

This C Program sorts the numbers in ascending order using bubble sort. Bubble sort is a simple sorting algorithm that works by repeatedly stepping through the list to be sorted, comparing each pair of adjacent items and swapping them if they are in the wrong order. Here we need to sort a number in ascending order.

```
void main()
{
int array[maxsize]; int i, j, num, temp;
printf("enter the value of num \n"); scanf("%d", &num);
```

```
printf("enter the elements one by one \n"); for (i = 0; i < num;
i++)
{
scanf("%d", &array[i]);
}
printf("input array is \n"); for (i = 0; i < num; i++)
{
printf("%d\n", array[i]);
}
/* bubble sorting begins */ for (i = 0; i < num; i++)
{
for (j = 0; j < (num - i - 1); j++)
{
if (array[j] > array[j + 1])
{
temp = array[j]; array[j] = array[j + 1]; array[j + 1] = temp;
}
}
}
printf("sorted array is...\n"); for (i = 0; i < num; i++)
{
printf("%d\n", array[i]);
}
}
```

Searching

Linear search in C programming: The following code implements linear search (Searching algorithm) which is used to find whether a given number is present in an array and if it is present then at what location it occurs. It is also known as sequential search

```
#include <stdio.h> int main()
{
int array[100], search, c, n;
printf("Enter the number of elements in array\n");
scanf("%d",&n);
```

```
printf("Enter %d integer(s)\n", n); for (c = 0; c < n; c++)
scanf("%d", &array[c]);
printf("Enter the number to search\n"); scanf("%d", &search);
for (c = 0; c < n; c++)
{
if (array[c] == search) /* if required element found */
{
printf("%d is present at location %d.\n", search, c+1); break;
}
}
if (c == n)
printf("%d is not present in array.\n", search);
return 0;
}
```

Enter the number of elements in array 5 Enter 5 numbers

12 23 35 71 50

Enter the number to search 71 71 is present at the location 4

CHAPTER FOUR

Pointers

Pointers

A pointer is a variable whose value is the address of another variable, i.e., direct address of the memory location. Like any variable or constant, you must declare a pointer before using it to store any variable address. The general form of a pointer variable declaration is –

type *var-name;

Here, type is the pointer's base type; it must be a valid C data type and var-name is the name of the pointer variable. The asterisk * used to declare a pointer is the same asterisk used for multiplication. However, in this statement the asterisk is being used to designate a variable as a pointer. Take a look at some of the valid pointer declarations –

int *ip; /* pointer to an integer */ double *dp; /* pointer to a double */ float *fp; /* pointer to a float */

char *ch /* pointer to a character */

The actual data type of the value of all pointers, whether integer, float, character, or otherwise, is the same, a long hexadecimal number that represents a memory address. The only difference between pointers of different data types is the data type of the variable or constant that the pointer points to.

Pointer to function

C programming allows passing a pointer to a function. To do so, simply declare the function parameter as a pointer type.

Following is a simple example where we pass an unsigned long pointer to a function and change the value inside the function which reflects back in the calling function –

The pointer in C language is a variable which stores the address of another variable. This variable can be of type int, char, array, function, or any other pointer. The size of the pointer depends on the architecture. However, in 32-bit architecture the size of a pointer is 2 byte.

Consider the following example to define a pointer which stores the address of an integer.

int n = 10;

int* p = &n; // Variable p of type pointer is pointing to the address of the variable n of type integer.

Declaring a pointer

The pointer in c language can be declared using * (asterisk symbol). It is also known as indirection pointer used to dereference a pointer.

int *a;//pointer to int

char *c;//pointer to char

Pointer Example

An example of using pointers to print the address and value is given below.

As you can see in the above figure, pointer variable stores the address of number variable, i.e., fff4. The value of number variable is 50. But the address of pointer variable p is aaa3.

By the help of * (indirection operator), we can print the value of pointer variable p.

#include<stdio.h>

int main(){

int number=50;

int *p;

p=&number;//stores the address of number variable

printf("Address of p variable is %x \n",p); // p contains the address of the number therefore printing p gives the address of number.

printf("Value of p variable is %d \n",*p); // As we know that * is used to dereference a pointer therefore if we print *p, we will get the value stored at the address contained by p.

return 0;

}

Pointer to array

int arr[10];

int *p[10]=&arr; // Variable p of type pointer is pointing to the address of an integer array arr.

Pointer to a function

void show (int);

void(*p)(int) = &display; // Pointer p is pointing to the address of a function

Pointer to structure

struct st {

int i;

float f;

}ref;

struct st *p = &ref;

Advantage of pointer

1) Pointer reduces the code and improves the performance, it is used to retrieving strings, trees, etc. and used with arrays, structures, and functions.

2) We can return multiple values from a function using the pointer.

3) It makes you able to access any memory location in the computer's memory.

Usage of pointer

There are many applications of pointers in c language.

1) Dynamic memory allocation

In c language, we can dynamically allocate memory using malloc() and calloc() functions where the pointer is used.

2) Arrays, Functions, and Structures

Pointers in c language are widely used in arrays, functions, and structures. It reduces the code and improves the performance.

Address Of (&) Operator

The address of operator '&' returns the address of a variable. But, we need to use %u to display the address of a variable.

```
#include<stdio.h>
int main(){
int number=50;
printf("value of number is %d, address of number is %u",number,&number);
return 0;
}
```

Output

value of number is 50, address of number is fff4

NULL Pointer

A pointer that is not assigned any value but NULL is known as the NULL pointer. If you don't have any address to be specified in the pointer at the time of declaration, you can assign NULL value. It will provide a better approach.

```
int *p=NULL;
```

In the most libraries, the value of the pointer is 0 (zero).

Pointer Program to swap two numbers without using the 3rd variable.

```
#include<stdio.h>
int main(){
int a=10,b=20,*p1=&a,*p2=&b;
printf("Before swap: *p1=%d *p2=%d",*p1,*p2);
*p1=*p1+*p2;
*p2=*p1-*p2;
*p1=*p1-*p2;
printf("\nAfter swap: *p1=%d *p2=%d",*p1,*p2);
return 0;
}
```

Output

Before swap: *p1=10 *p2=20 After swap: *p1=20 *p2=10

Reading complex pointers

There are several things which must be taken into the consideration while reading the complex pointers in C. Lets see the precedence and associativity of the operators which are used regarding pointers.

Here,we must notice that,

(): This operator is a bracket operator used to declare and define the function.

[]: This operator is an array subscript operator

* : This operator is a pointer operator.

Identifier: It is the name of the pointer. The priority will always be assigned to this.

Data type: Data type is the type of the variable to which the pointer is intended to point. It also includes the modifier like signed int, long, etc).

How to read the pointer: int (*p)[10].

To read the pointer, we must see that () and [] have the equal precedence. Therefore, their associativity must be considered here. The associativity is left to right, so the priority goes to ().

Inside the bracket (), pointer operator * and pointer name (identifier) p have the same precedence. Therefore, their associativity must be considered here which is right to left, so the priority goes to p, and the second priority goes to *.

Assign the 3rd priority to [] since the data type has the last precedence. Therefore the pointer will look like following.

char -> 4

* -> 2

p -> 1

[10] -> 3

The pointer will be read as p is a pointer to an array of integers of size 10.

CHAPTER FIVE

C - FILE I/O

C - FILE I/O

The last chapter explained the standard input and output devices handled by C programming language. This chapter cover how C programmers can create, open, close text or binary files for their data storage.

A file represents a sequence of bytes, regardless of it being a text file or a binary file. C programming language provides access on high level functions as well as low

level OSlevelOSlevel calls to handle file on your storage devices. This chapter will take you through the important calls for file management.

Opening Files

You can use the **fopen** function to create a new file or to open an existing file. This call will initialize an object of the type **FILE**, which contains all the information necessary to control the stream. The prototype of this function call is as follows –

FILE *fopen(const char * filename, const char * mode);

Here, **filename** is a string literal, which you will use to name your file, and access **mode** can have one of the following values –

r - Opens an existing text file for reading purpose.

w- Opens a text file for writing. If it does not exist, then a new file is created. Here your program will start writing content from the beginning of the file.

a - Opens a text file for writing in appending mode. If it does not exist, then a new file is created. Here your program will start appending content in the existing file content.

r+ Opens a text file for both reading and writing.

w+ Opens a text file for both reading and writing. It first truncates the file to zero length if it exists, otherwise creates a file if it does not exist.

a+ Opens a text file for both reading and writing. It creates the file if it does not exist. The reading will start from the beginning but writing can only be appended.

Closing a File

To close a file, use the fclose function. The prototype of this function is –

int fclose(FILE *fp);

The **fclose**-- function returns zero on success, or EOF if there is an error in closing the file. This function actually flushes any data still pending in the buffer to the file, closes the file, and releases any memory used for the file. The EOF is a constant defined in the header file stdio.h.

There are various functions provided by C standard library to read and write a file, character by character, or in the form of a fixed length string.

Writing a File

Following is the simplest function to write individual characters to a stream –

int fputc(int c, FILE *fp);

The function fputc writes the character value of the argument c to the output stream referenced by fp. It returns the written character written on success otherwise EOF if there is an error. You can use the following functions to write a null-terminated string to a stream –

int fputs(const char *s, FILE *fp);

The function fputs writes the string s to the output stream referenced by fp. It returns a non- negative value on success, otherwise EOF is returned in case of any error. You can use int fprintfFILE∗fp,constchar∗format,...FILE∗fp,constchar∗format,... function as well to write a string into a file. Try the following example.

Make sure you have /tmp directory available. If it is not, then before proceeding, you must create this directory on your machine.

```
#include <stdio.h> main() {
FILE *fp;
fp = fopen("/tmp/test.txt", "w+"); fprintf(fp, "This is testing for fprintf...\n"); fputs("This is testing for fputs...\n", fp); fclose(fp);
}
```

When the above code is compiled and executed, it creates a new file test.txt in /tmp directory and writes two lines using two different functions. Let us read this file in the next section.

Reading a File

Given below is the simplest function to read a single character from a file –

int fgetc(FILE * fp);

The fgetc function reads a character from the input file referenced by fp. The return value is the character read, or in case of any error, it returns EOF. The following function allows to read a string from a stream –

char *fgets(char *buf, int n, FILE *fp);

The functions fgets reads up to n-1 characters from the input stream referenced by fp. It copies the read string into the buffer buf, appending a null character to terminate the string.

If this function encounters a newline character '\n' or the end of the file EOF before they have read the maximum number of characters, then it returns only the characters read up to that point including the new line character. You can also use int fscanfFILE∗fp,constchar∗format,...FILE∗fp,constchar∗format,... function to read strings from a file, but it stops reading after encountering the first space character.

```
#include <stdio.h> main() {
FILE *fp;
char buff[255];
```

fp = fopen("/tmp/test.txt", "r"); fscanf(fp, "%s", buff);

printf("1 : %s\n", buff); fgets(buff, 255, (FILE*)fp); printf("2: %s\n", buff); fgets(buff, 255, (FILE*)fp); printf("3: %s\n", buff); fclose(fp);

}

When the above code is compiled and executed, it reads the file created in the previous section and produces the following result –

1 : This

2: is testing for fprintf...

3: This is testing for fputs...

Let's see a little more in detail about what happened here. First, fscanf read just This because after that, it encountered a space, second call is for fgets which reads the remaining line till it encountered end of line. Finally, the last call fgets reads the second line completely.

Binary I/O Functions

There are two functions, that can be used for binary input and output –

size_t fread(void *ptr, size_t size_of_elements, size_t number_of_elements, FILE *a_file);

size_t fwrite(const void *ptr, size_t size_of_elements, size_t number_of_elements, FILE *a_file);

Both of these functions should be used to read or write blocks of memories - usually arrays or structures.

Random Access to File

There is no need to read each record sequentially, if we want to access a particular record.C supports these functions for random access file processing.

1. fseek()
2. ftell()
3. rewind()

fseek():

This function is used for seeking the pointer position in the file at the specified byte.

Syntax: fseek(file pointer, displacement, pointer position);

Where

file pointer ---- It is the pointer which points to the file. **displacement** ---- It is positive or negative.This is the number of bytes which are skipped backward (if negative) or forward(if positive) from the current position.This is attached with L because this is a long integer.

ftell()

This function returns the value of the current pointer position in the file.The value is count from the beginning of the file.

CHAPTER SIX

MCQ

_____ is a picture in which the flows of computational paths are depicted.

(A) Algorithm
(B) Program
(C) Code
(D) Flow chart

Among unary operation which operator represents increment?

(A) --
(B) ++
(C) -
(D) !

The function scanf is used to ____

(A) To take logical decisions
(B) Input a set of values
(C) Print a set of values
(D) Do mathematical manipulations

If the function returns no value then it is called _____

(A) Data type function
(B) Calling function
(C) Main function
(D) Void function

A function ______

(A) May or may not need input data
(B) May or may not return a value
(C) Both a and b

(D) None of these

Which character is used to indicate the end of the string?

(A) Any alphabet

(B) A

(C) Null

(D) None of these

Each element of a structure can be _____

(A) Read and printed as a separate data item

(B) Printed as a separate data item

(C) Read as a separate data item

(D) None of these

In the for loop structure, which statement is present?

(A) Assign statement

(B) Alter statement

(C) Both (a) and (b)

(D) None of these

When the computer is waiting for the input?

(A) Files are selected

(B) The cursor is blinking in the VDU screen

(C) Menu will appear on the screen

(D) None of these

Which can be included in a string constant using the escape sequences?

(A) Apostrophe (')

(B) Question mark (?)

(C) Double quotes (")

(D) All the above

9 798887 727608

Printed by Libri Plureos GmbH in Hamburg,
Germany